TO KISS THE SOUL OF A WOMAN

by

Martice S. Hanible

TO KISS THE SOUL OF A WOMAN

Copyright © 2011 by MARTICE S. HANIBLE

ISBN-10 0984744436
ISBN-13 978-0-9847444-3-5

All rights reserved. No part of this book may be reproduced or transmitted in any form or by any means without written permission of the author.

Any comments may be directed to the author:

MARTICE S. HANIBLE #K70069
Hill Correction Center
POBox 1700
Galesburg IL 61402

Special contributors:
Willie James Williams
Jackie (Jack Black) Kelly

Published by:
Midnight Express Books
POBox 69
Berryville AR 72616

ACKNOWLEDGEMENTS

To my daughter, Matrice Lashay Hanible; Princess, I love you and I want you to know that you are literally your father's reason for living.

To my Mother, Shirley Jean Collins, I love you lil' woman!

To my Grandma, Muddy Jean Collins; thank you for financially and emotionally contributing to me becoming a published author/poet.

To my guy, Jackie Kelly, (Jack Black). A straight and thorough street fellow who gave me the bulk of the finance for this work of art. Even though you're a Street Kat and all you knew me to be was a Street Kat. But regardless, you supported your Brotha in this venture. Man, it ain't nothin' but love, Brotha.

To all my family and friends supporting me through this hardship of imprisonment.

And, to my Father; with you as my Father, I am able to be the gentleman I am. So, thank you, Pops . . .

Contents

I WANT TO GET TO KNOW YOU	1
BONDS OF AFFECTION	3
I EQUALS YOU	4
BABY, LET'S FALL IN LOVE	5
TO KISS THE SOUL OF A WOMAN	6
A WOMAN'S SACRIFICE	8
I'm Lost Inside of You	9
I Am Not Him	10
You Were Made to Be Loved	11
A Valentine's Day Date (With Martice Hanible)	12
She's Mamako, She's Queen, She's Reyna	13
A Good Man	14
Dear Mother	15
No Title (Mother's Day)	16
No Title (Mothers' Day II)	17
My Ageless Goddess	18
Would You Mind	19
"If I Only Had One Night to Love You"	21
She's Just Perfect	22
Happy Valentine's Day	23
My Inspiration Part I	24
My Inspiration Part II	25
She Kissed Me Part I	26
She Kissed Me Part II	27

Who Truly Loves Her 28

The Man Who Loves You 29

My Winnie Medela, My Coretta Scott King, My Betty Shabazz 31

Goddess Stand on Your Cloud 33

You're Worth More Than You Think 34

While Standing Strong She's Beautiful 35

When Heaven Touches Earth 37

I Dream to Touch You 38

Today I Vow 40

Dear Young Madre 42

Stand Strong Princess 43

As a Man Thinketh 44

To My Extended Essence 45

Before I Pass Away 46

Why Does She Fear 47

Lonely Nights and Saddened Days 48

I Never Knew Who You Were (Until I Lost You) 50

Open Your Heart (and Let Me Enter) 51

I Came to Restore You 53

Will She Ever Have the Chance To Love Her Soul mate 54

Finding Our 7th Heaven 55

May I Kiss Those Tears Away 56

I Just Want to Make Love to You 58

About The Author 59

I WANT TO GET TO KNOW YOU

Excuse me, Miss Lady
I don't intend to interrupt what you're doing,
But my eyes are attracted to what they see,
And what they see is your outer beauty,
I don't want to sound all corny,
And I ain't the one to run no game,
Plus, I know you done heard it all.
The truth is Princess,
I hesitated to approach you,
But, I couldn't let this opportunity pass,
Because I might come to regret it.
Thinking about the what is and what ain't,
What could've been and what should've been
What could be and what should be,
All speculations with no answers,
Left with only the what if's.
I don't know if you have a man, a friend, or an associate,
I know you're not married because I don't see no ring,
But, again, I may be wrong — you may be getting it appraised.
I saw your smile,
And I said, "Man, that girl's beautiful!"
I kept lusting, I ain't gon' lie,
Then I caught your eyes,
And they made me want to get to know you.
They got the sparkle of the sunlight striking a blue diamond.
It attracts you,
It pulls you in,
It makes you want it in a way — that until you see it you never knew.
And I know you've run across a lot of guys,
That used this line,
"I want to get to know you."
But, I done already been there before,
Been there, done that,
Princess, I ain't getting no younger, so I ain't got no time to be lying.
Right now, I'm truthfully looking for someone more than a shell,
More than something to look at,

To Kiss The Soul Of A Woman

More than someone to get on, or get under,
I'm looking for a companion.
A friend, a guide, when I'm going in the wrong direction,
An emergency search team to find me when I'm lost,
And bring me to safety.
I'm looking for the one who — when I'm down, she gon' pick me up,
When I'm too weak to walk on my own — she gon' be my crutch.
One that when the world is on my shoulders and it's too much for me to bear,
She gon' take it off mine's and put it on her's;
A woman who'll appreciate me when the situation is visa versa.
What good would it be, Princess — to have a shell with no substance,
It's a beautiful decoration, but other than that it serves no purpose.
I want a woman that — if her appearance changes, my love stays the same.
And the only way I could do that, Princess,
Is if I learn to love her, and not her shell.
I want to get to know you . . .
I want to get to know if your inner beauty is as extravagant as your outer.
I want to know if your smile reflects the shine of your heart.
I want to know — that if the eyes are a reflection of your soul — is your soul that amazing!!!
I want to get to know if your heart could reflect the same beauty as your eyes reflect;
If not greater,
Princess . . .
I want to get to know you.

Date: 7-04-04
Place; Statesville C.C.
Hour: Around 3:00 A.M.
Reason: Trying to go to rest, but thinking about poetry after hearing poetry spoken on Apollo,(M.C. "Steve Harvey," on Channel 9.

BONDS OF AFFECTION

Time and space may separate us
But true love has the ability to take us
On a journey beyond the physical
And embrace the mental.
We travel the miles of turmoil together
And withstand the obstacles together.
Sacrifices we make will reward our future
As short lived struggles will strengthen our relations.
A thought of submission is never an option,
For weakness has no place in true love relationships.
Life is a treasure worth fighting for,
And love is life's stronghold.
We live to enjoy the fruits of our labor,
And bask in the beauty of our sacrifices.
We remember the sacrifices of the other,
In which bring us to this point;
And make us strong enough
to maintain our love.
As I reminisce on your strengths and you
On mine's,
Our bonds of affection ignites the remedy that withstood the tests of time.
For we learned that time is not a strong
Enough element to break the bonds of
Affection that we call . . .Love

Date: 12-18-07
Place: Danville C.C.
Inspiration: A conversation Mustapha had with his wife (girl).

I EQUALS YOU

Together we are a balance,
A balance of male and female companionship.
A scale of justice as the Kemitic Goddess, Maat,
A scale which balances male and female energy, keeping
the world steady even while rotating oblonged.
We are creation; one with the other.
Two energy life-forces connecting to make both one.
Two souls intertwined,
Two thoughts making us one mind.
Two purposes flourishing to meet one agenda,
Two human beings copulating to create one potential.
Our balance makes us an essential element
That illustrates our two worlds as one Heaven.
Our lives as one question,
Our answers as one existence.
Our imbalance is unfathomable,
For you could never separate the two,
For I equals you . . .

Date: 8-24-07
Place: Danville C.C.
Inspiration: Having a conversation with Ya-Ya, (John-John), about a female, and this thought just popped up.

BABY, LET'S FALL IN LOVE

Baby, I know that you love me,
But, there's a new journey I ask you to take with me
 Baby, just fall in love with me.
(name)
And I know it's strange for me to ask such a thing,
But, you're my dream;
And I've fallen in love with you,
And I just want you to fall in love with me, too.
And you don't have to answer me today
But when time permits me to be there
Would you let me know then, if you have?
Baby, let's fall in love . . .

Date: 1-02-08
Place: Danville C.C. Cell house/cell
4B-16
Inspiration: Listening to Isley Brothers, "Let's Fall In Love"
on the "Beautiful Ballads tape . . ."

TO KISS THE SOUL OF A WOMAN

To kiss the soul of a woman'
And to make love to her emotions;
Is to turn the quietest whisper into the gentlest of touches.
A sensitive thought every once in a while,
Takes her mind state back to that of a child's,
An innocent thought from a woman creates the innocent action,
And gives her a satisfying feeling that makes her heart smile . . .

To kiss the soul of a woman,
And to make love to her emotions;
Is the bare walks in the rain, when you stop, stand, stare, and talk,
To come home to sit in the window to listen to the soft taps on the glass as the rain drops.
To smell the freshness of Mother Nature's most fabulous creations,
To hear the wind whistle, to feel the soothing breeze through the cracks,
is such a lovely sensation . . .

To kiss the soul of a woman
And to make love to her emotions;
Is to hold her hand in front of a crowd of millions.
To stop traffic in the middle of the busiest street, to give her a slow dance,
To take a chance and make love to her in a field with the sweet aroma of flowers,
Which started as a picnic and turned into a romance . . .

To kiss the soul of a woman,
And to make love to her emotions;
Is to watch the sun set into the waves of the ocean.
To walk along the shore of the beach,
To feel the sand grains beneath your feet;
To tell her wonderful words that'll take her breath away.
That leave her without a single word to speak.

To kiss the soul of a woman'
And to make love to her emotions;

Martice S. Hanible

Is to call and awake her in the midst of her sleep to tell her that you love her;
And to assure her that by you she's wanted.
To interrupt her between the busiest hours of the day,
To have delivered to her a Teddy Bear, chocolate candy, and her favorite bouquet.
To make her temperature rise,
By making love to her mind.
To kiss the soul of a woman,
And make love to her emotions;
It's a beautiful thing . . .

Date: 4-24-01
Place: Statesville E-728
To Isley Brothers — Don't Say Goodbye

A WOMAN'S SACRIFICE

She eats last after she feeds her husband and children
She sleeps last after she tends to her family and her household
She weeps little, for after her hard days toil, her tears have no
Energy to fall
She smiles even when she's sad to make others happy
She sacrifices her health and happiness to keep her family's health
And happiness.
She goes hungry at night to feed her husband and children
She goes without sufficient clothing to clothe her family.
She'll give her life to protect our lives
She dies inside so that we'll live
This is a woman's sacrifice
But, is she ever appreciated for it?

> Date: 3-30-0
> Time: 1:50 P.M.
> Place: Danville C.C.

Inspiration: Watching a wildlife movie with a female fox feeding her pups; even though she's starving . . . This made me think about women.

I'm Lost Inside of You

Every day, my needs grow stronger for you,
You've become my need to reach...my need to walk,
You've captured me with your inner beauty,
You've seduced me with your loving personality.
Your kindness encases my interest,
Your strength capsules my weaknesses.
I'm simply lost inside of you...

(name)
We slow dance with our hearts,
We make love without a touch.
We flirt without a word spoken,
We vacation through paper and imagination,
Without even knowing our souls are no longer two,

(name), I'm simply lost inside of you...
Our auras stretch 900 miles to meet one another,
They walk hand in hand to comfort each other.
Our spirits rise,
To meet in their skies,
our minds combine,
Becoming stronger, becoming more wise.
We are coupled with our destiny, for we are no longer two,

(name), I'm simply lost inside of you...

Date: 2-07-08
Place: Danville C.C.
Reason: For Rina for Valentine's Day

I Am Not Him

I'm not him baby,
I'm not the man who made you feel less than the wonderful
Woman that you are;
I'm not the man that made you feel unworthy of true love.
I haven't betrayed your trust,
And I haven't done you wrong.
Baby, I am me...
I am not him...

I'm not him baby,
I'm not the man who physically, emotionally and
Mentally abused you;
I'm not the man who degraded, down played and
Discouraged you.
I'm not the man who failed to understand your true value.
I haven't underestimated your worth,
And I haven't done you wrong.
Baby, I am me...
I am not him...

I'm not him baby,
I didn't take your kindness for a weakness;
I didn't hurt your feelings by not supporting you.
I haven't neglected to comfort and endorse you,
And I have done you no wrong.
For baby, I am me...
I am not him...

Date: 3-28-08
Place: Danville C.C. 4B-16
Inspiration: Listening to O'Jays' song, "You and Me"

You Were Made to Be Loved

You were made to be loved,
And I--I was made to love you...

> Date: 2-03-05
> Place: Stateville C.C. Cell/Cellhouse D-554
> Reason: Just because

A Valentine's Day Date (With Martice Hanible)

It's February 14th, 2008.
It's getting late so you wonder if I've remembered you.
Your eyes welled with tears at their corners,
You're beginning to feel lonely, unappreciated, unwanted.
Not knowing what your man has planned,
You surprisingly feel someone grab your hands
And hug you from behind.
He kisses the sides of your neck and whispers a word in your ear...
"Upstairs"
What's there, is flirtation--or shall I say appreciation
From your better half.
The tips of the stairs are candle lit,
Velvet flooring comforts the soles of your feet.
Bath water awaits you,
As your man undresses then bathes you.
He dries you with an elegant cloth
So soft that it relaxes your thoughts.
He dresses you in a dress and high heels of your favorite color, He's
so familiar with your bodies contours that your new dress fits
Your curves just perfect.
As your hands are merged into his, he guides you into a room
Fitted with an orchestra surrounding a dinner table just for you.
As the orchestra begins with melodies that are so familiar,
He stands, as a mic is passed and he sings to you your favorite love Song.
Your eyes are deluged in water as your tears begin to fall,
You two cry together but--he cries not only with his tears but too
Through the words of this song.
He kisses you softly as you talk under the candle light...
And although tonight he wants to make love to you physically,
He choose only ... to make love to you mentally.
This, Princess, is a Valentine's Day date with Martice Hanible.
Happy Valentine's Day....

Date: 1-10-08
Place: Danville C.C. 4B16
Reason: To place on web page for Valentine's Day, to romance women
mentally with word and not physical.

She's Mamako, She's Queen, She's Reyna

She's royalty,
She's the feminine quality of a king.
She sets not on his left, but on his right hand side,
For she's divinity.
She's the silent advisor,
The hidden strength of the throne.
She's the focus keeper of the kingdom,
The regenerator of the royal bloodline.
She's the key component that makes the land function,
For she is wiser than most;
For her heart, her mind and her soul are aligned with
The stars.
She's cosmically at one with the Author of creation,
She's allotted to her masculine better half as a
Gift from the Supreme Being.
In Ki-Swahili, she's addressed as Mamako,
In English, she's addressed as Queen,
In Spanish, she's addressed as Reyna...

Date: 9-21-07
Place: Danville C.C.
Inspiration: thinking about Rina('s) middle name, "Reyna"

A Good Man

Never judge a book by its cover.
A good man doesn't just come with a smile and physical freedom. Sometimes he comes with his heart filled with agony and pain. Sometimes he's covered deeper in the ground and dirt than an unpolished diamond, but he has all the potential in the world to be discovered, polished and beautiful.

Date: May or June of 2007
Place: Danville C.C. 1C-79

Dear Mother

Dear Mother,
    Time has never erased
    The boundless affection of
    Your love, to your son. And circumstances has
    Never placed a limitation
    Upon your support and
    Your love.
        It's like we're inseparable
From the core...
    I mean...
    You're baring the stretch
    Marks that are an
    Indication of my being.
    You were the first one
    To love me,
    To hug me,
    To kiss me,
    To nurture me,
    To speak to me while
    I lay in your womb.
You are my shining star...
You are the rock
That I know will
 Still be there
Whenever I return.
You are one I can
Count on to be
There when all others
Have gone.

You are...my
Replacement to the sun...
          HAPPY MOTHER'S DAY

Date: April 18, 2010
Place: Stateville C.C. (F-338)
Reason: For my mother Shirley Jean Collins for Mothers' Day.

No Title (Mother's Day)

There isn't ever a moment
When I'd stand alone
Without you by my side.
A time when I may be
An embarrassment to others
But to you...
I'm still Your pride.
A time when my best
Is not enough, but
Your love makes it suffice,
When all else goes wrong
But your words make all
Seem right.

For you are the cause
Of my life
The reason for my birth;
The first oxygen that I breathed
The first beat to my heart.
So on this day,
I give you thanks...

    HAPPY MOTHERS' DAY

          Date: May 5, 2010
        Place: Stateville C.C. (F-338)
     Reason: For Nickelboy's mother for Mothers' Day

No Title (Mothers' Day II)

So many years we face
The world alone,
Always trying to find
That special someone
To call our own.
To make a house a home,
We--somehow fall in
Love,
Thinking we'd make everything
Right in our lives that's wrong.

So many times we fail
To understand that love
Feeds life
And life is a joy worth Nurturing.

Forever in a day
We fail to recall to appreciate,
The life that gave us faith,
And the life that gave her (our daughter)
Birth on that beautiful
Winters' date.

So many opportunities we
Simply walk by...
Not refusing but ineffectively
Acknowledging the mother
That gave birth to our child,
But not right now...
For today...
I must say.... (name),
           HAPPY MOTHERS' DAY

                    Date: May 5, 2010
              Place: Stateville C.C. (F-338)
Reason: For Nickelboy's daughters' mother for Mothers' Day

My Ageless Goddess

Dear Gorgeous,
My ageless goddess;
As eons travel, your beauty stands still,
And your smile still shines as a precious
Diamond under an
African sun ray.

Your eyes still gleam
That childish glare of
Youth and innocence.
And your laughter,
So sweet, tickles the
Very fiber of the
Earth and compliments
My every heartbeat.

You are a jewel
That crystallizes,
Fine wine that ferments,
The love song that is
Forever hummed.
You are the vibrations
That ages not,
And the time that is
Forever young.
You are...my ageless
Goddess....

     "HAPPY BIRTHDAY"

          Date: 4-15-10
        Place: Stateville C.C. F-338
      Reason: For Sunshine's Birthday

Would You Mind

Baby would you mind,
    If I was the man that you met
    In your childhood years;
    The man that you dreamed of
    Spending the rest of your Life with?
    The childhood crush that
    Lasted forever and a day;
    That schoolyard fling
    That turned into a life long
    Romance?

Baby would you mind,
    If I was the first man to ever
    Hold your hand;
    And kiss your palms?
    The first man to ask for the
    Last dance;
    When the lights are low and
    The music's real slow, and I whisper in your ear...
    "Baby, can I be your man"?

Baby would you mind,
    If I made you my fairytale Princess
    To have you take a seat and
    Place glass slippers on your Feet?
    To caress your cheek with the
    Back of my finger tips;
    And to catch your falling
    Tears before they're ever
    Released?

Baby would you mind,
    If I grew older with you
    and still told you that I
    Loved you every waking day;
    Still kiss you good night

To Kiss The Soul Of A Woman

And to wake in the morning
With you waking by my side...
Every day is what I'd pray?
Still look into your eyes
And find that you make me
Love you even more;
And still watch you as you
Walk away...still
Whispering...
"Tu bonita mi amor"
(Your still beautiful my love)?
Baby would you mind....

Date: 3-29-10
Place: Stateville C.C. F-338
Reason: Thinking of the song
Information: "Would You Mind", by Earth, Wind and Fire

"If I Only Had One Night to Love You"

If I only had one night to love you,
I'd want more than an occasional physical.
I'd want more than to hug and touch you,
I'd want to sit in front of a fireplace, sip wine with you
And just talk with you.

If I only had one night to love you,
I'd listen to every single word that belongs to you.
I wouldn't waste a moment's time not appreciating your mind.
I'd understand that every second of my being with you
Is much more valuable than the last.

If I only had one night to love you,
I'd spend the night enjoying your presence.
For tonight I wouldn't want to be anyone other than
Who I am,
As I wouldn't want you to be anyone other than who you are.
And that's if, I only had one night ...to love you...

Date: 3-14-08
Place: Danville C.C. 4B-16
Inspiration: Watching T.V. show "Gone Country on channel 51". Bobby Brown, Sisco and other stars had to write a country song to see who could be the next big country star.

She's Just Perfect

She's wondrously gorgeous in many men eyes,
She's a bundle of perfection but her perfection she denies.
She's wondering why I love her and touch her in every
Imaginable way,
She's secretly insecure about her thighs, her breasts,
Her waist.
She doesn't know about her stretched marked stomach
Being her perfection.
For she gave birth to an angel, therefore her stomach
Housed a heaven.
She doesn't know that her thick thighs are a man's dream,
Her eyes are reflecting gems,
And her lips are made to be kissed.
She doesn't know rather she's slim or thick.
In many men eyes...
She's just perfect.

> Date: 8-14-07
> Place: Danville C.C.
> Time: 11:28 P.M.
> Reason: For women who's insecure with their body image
> Inspiration: Tyra Banks talk show about this subject

Happy Valentine's Day

My essence lies within my goddess,
My comfort lies within her understanding me,
My solace lies within her love and
My strength lies within her confidence in me...
Rina,
Today we celebrate this
Happy Valentine's Day
"07"

Date: 2-14-07
Place: Danville C.C.
Inspiration: Writing a piece for Rina for Valentines' Day

My Inspiration Part I

Combined was two genres completely opposite;
Both souls compromising, both
Spirits now one breath.
Fantastically molded, wonderfully blessed;
Wonderous angel, earthly godness.
Sweetest of nectar, scent of a peach;
As marvelous as a spring flower, as great as
An unadulterous stream.
Soothing as Marvin Gaye's whispers, in the middle
Of the night;
Definitely my inspiration, unquestionably a
Delight to life.

Date: 10-14-00
Time: 12-afternoon/colliente time
Mood: Cool
Place: S.C.C. 2A-08 I-House-Seg.
Reason: For Martrice Lashay Hanible (My child, my daughter)

My Inspiration Part II

I never had a love like this before,
Straight from me, my seed for sho.
Smile Sunshine, my princess, young queen;
My everything, smile for its happiness you've
Given me.
I've now found a reason to live, a reason to smile.
My child, for a long while I've awaited this
Feeling;
The missing peace to the puzzle, you've now fulfilled
It.
And now that I'm down, & thought to be out;
The time when all have abandoned, and
Laughters loud.
You keep me fighting, keep my head
Held high.
You are for surely my inspiration, I cannot deny.

> Date: 10-15-00
> Time: About 2:00 P.M.
> Mood: Feeling alright
> Place: S.C.C. Seg. I-house 2A-08
> Reason: For Martrice--my daughter
> Part II

She Kissed Me Part I

She kissed a kiss, that'll last a lifetime.
She held a hold, that'll be felt forever.
She softly speaks a word in a voice that resonates
Through infinity.
She breathes a breath that tastes as sweet as the
Ripest plum tree.
She kissed a kiss, that'll last a lifetime.

Date: 7-14-08
Place: Danville C.C. 4B-16
Inspiration: In class "The Humanities Through the Arts", watching a movie about Romeo and Juliet. Romeo tells Juliet, "Let our lips do what our hands do", (Which was kiss. She kissed his hand with her hand [Palm to palm]

She Kissed Me Part II

Her lips felt, as soft as the softest flower pelts.
They are as pink as the palm of an infants' hand.
She held a hold that'll be felt forever.
We embraced, as if we were the clouds and the sky.
Her flesh is, as soft as the feathers of a canary
She softly speaks a word in a voice that resonates
Through infinity.
Her words are harmonious,
Her voice is as harps of fascinated melody.
She breathes a breath that tastes, as sweet as the
Ripest plum tree
Her speech brushes my eye lids,
With breath as gentle as a rain drop melts.
She kissed a kiss, that'll last a lifetime.
She held a hold, that'll last forever.
She softly speaks a word in a voice that resonates
Through infinity.
She breathes a breath that tastes, as sweet as the
Ripest plum tree.
She kissed a kiss, that'll last a lifetime.
She kissed me--as I dreamed...

> Date: 7-14-08
> Place: Danville C.C. 4B-16
> Inspiration: In class watching Romeo and Juliet

Who Truly Loves Her

A man who truly loves her,
Is the man who will appreciate
The very least of her.

Date: 12-12-07
Place: Danville C.C. Cell/house 4B-16
Inspiration: Rina, friend broke up with her undeserving (of her) boyfriend but has found another guy who she thinks is love...

The Man Who Loves You

The man who loves you
For the way you look
Will leave you
For the same,
When you change,
From what he wants
Or when you change,
Just because you age...

The man who loves you
For the way you make love
To him,
Will leave you for the same,
When he gets tired
Or it gets bored
With the way your hips sway.

The man who loves you
For what you can do for him (monetarily),
Will leave you for the same.
When you can do no more,
When you have to be less,
He'll find someone else
To take your place.

The man who loves you
Because you're you...
Will love you till the
Day you expire,
He'll take you higher
Than you've ever been before,
Because every day as you
Get better as his girl
He'll love you even more...

And that's the man who loves you...

To Kiss The Soul Of A Woman

Date: 5-30-10
Place: Hill C.0 4B-58
Inspiration: Movie, Medea's Family Union (Poetry segment in club).

My Winnie Medela, My Coretta Scott King, My Betty Shabazz

My Winnie Mendela
I'm just writing to tell you
Of the things I've been through
and things you've helped me through.
I'm just writing to let you know,
That your words and your visits warmed my soul
While I was living in that jail cell of a hell hole.
You fought our fight taking on the leadership role to
Yourself
As if I was still there.
Kept our family strong,
At the same time fighting to keep liberated my
Incarcerated soul...
My wife Winnie Mendela,
You stood by me,
You stood strong...

My Corretta Scott King,
You too had a dream
And you lived your dream through me.
You edged me on
At times that I wanted to give up.
You loved our struggle
But still you supported your man and allowed him to
Stand out front.
Pushed your independent dreams and solutions to the
People through my words, but they were your
Thoughts.
I wonder how many people in the world knew,
That I was a reflection of you,
Just as you are a reflection of I...

My Betty Shabazz
My love who chose to fall in love

To Kiss The Soul Of A Woman

With a once upon a time street thug.
So strong, so pure at heart, so eloquent, so intelligent
Stood by my side when I laid undecided.
Spent time to find myself
Travelled 9,000 miles to find myself.
And when I got back
You were the other half of me
That stood right beside me
Searching too--to help find me...

My love, my queen, my destiny
You are my Winnie Mendela, my Corretta Scott King, my
Betty Shabazz...
My Winnie Mendela, my Corretta Scott King,
My Betty Shabazz...

Date: 5-01-07
Place: Danville C.C.
Inspiration: John John and his buddy Tawanna, talked about these women on a visit.

Goddess Stand on Your Cloud

Goddess, stand on your cloud,
Stand in your skies and rise and set your sun.
Create your rain to irrigate your crop of the world and its' children. To
watch them bloom and regenerate--
Repopulating the material matter that's called earth revolving and
Evolving in space...

Goddess, stand on your cloud.
Stand as an emblem princess,
As a symbol of endurance,
Let your goddess status stand as a representation to the children,
That as you stand strong and endure, life is what you make it.
Stand goddess and bow to the man that kneels before your feet.
Look down at your creation
And understand your greatness,
Understand that without you nothing that exists could have ever
Existed.
Never sit idle with your head hung low...
For you--are the cause of it all.

So goddess, stand on your cloud...

Date: 11-23-07
Place: Danville C.C. 4B-16
Inspiration: Just a thought about women who should know their goddess status :-)

You're Worth More Than You Think

(name), you're worth more than what you
Think you deserve,
You're worth more than any fantasy you've ever had.
You're worth more than human perfection,
Which is perfection only God could prepare to give.

Date: 7-09-07
Place: Danville C.C.
Reason: In response to a letter Rina wrote me. This was part of my letter in response.
Inspiration: Rina Reyna Hernandez letter to me 6-28-07

While Standing Strong She's Beautiful

While standing strong she's beautiful,
She's had more trials than you or I would know.
She's been raised in a world where men try to suppress her, Still she shares the feministic views of women who have become bitter.
Instead of hating all men she simply saves her body,
Patiently awaiting to give it as a gift to a man she knows Will genuinely respect, honor, cherish, and love her. That's why, while standing strong she's beautiful. :-)

She stared at the world being a single mother of
Four children
No child support, on public aid and haven't heard a
Word from her childrens' father
She awakes early in the mornings to perform her
Motherly duties,
She jots off to work, but as she comes home, she
Has to stop off at the church and stand in line to
Except from them free food.
She's struggling to make it, but she's making it,
She goes to rest hungry at night, because she sacrifices
Her own meals to make sure that her children are
Properly fed.
And that's why, while standing strong she's beautiful.

She protests what she believes is wrong,
She stands against it by protest, poems, and songs. She writes books, speaks out at forums,
She teaches at penitentiaries, alternate schools, and Host T.V. shows.
She argues intelligently when she's actually one who Speaks silently.
She's not one who's afraid to speak her mind when her Opposers threaten to act violently,
She's the one whom I wish was one with me...
Because--, while standing strong she's beautiful.

Date: 6-12-07
Place: Danville C.C.

To Kiss The Soul Of A Woman

Time: 11:05 A.M.
Reason: For women who stand for what they believe in and fight through a struggle
Inspiration: Looking at "Final Call" newspaper today, watching a sister on a real estate show last night and think about single mothers some special teachers and a female (Rina) I know.

When Heaven Touches Earth

When the feet of Heaven touches Earth;
Grass greens and, carnations bloom,
Children play and, toddlers grow.
Fire hydrates bustle, with the laughter of
The young,
Innocence shines brightly, suppressing the dawn.
When the feet of Heaven touches the Earth;
Constantly birds sing from the tree tops,
Motherly aromas escape the kitchen windows and,
Fatherly advice is being shared among the
Young ones.

When the feet of Heaven touches Earth;
Gloomy days are now vibrant,
Cries turn into smiles,
Rain turns into sunshine,
And hung heads are now held high.
When the feet of Heaven touches Earth;
We finally realize "that Heaven" is a wife
That Heaven is you...

Date: 7-19-08
Place: Danville C.C. 4B-16
Inspiration: Heard something on T.V. last night about Heaven touching Earth, for Rina birthday.

I Dream to Touch You

She's a rose that grew from the concrete,
Of the hard core Chicago streets.
Her heart beats love as her mind fantasizes,
About the possibilities of a greater life.
She dreams as a dreamer--her thoughts constantly
Expanding,
Her aspiration pushes her towards putting forth
The effort,
But her eyes reminds her of the harsh realities,
Of the possibilities of her dying before she
Makes this all happens;
She fears getting old and being physically unable
To enjoy this fantasy life that she tried hard
To make happen.
She dreams of being loved by her knight
Riding her off into the sunset on his white horse,
She dreams of being loved not for her external
Beauty, but for the greatness she houses
Inside of her heart...
And that's all that she wants.
She dreams of traveling to Africa and grooming
Her son to be an humanitarian who's ethnically
Diverse,
She dreams of the day in which she could be touched;
A touch not synonymous for making love to her
Physically,
A touch that erects her spiritually and exalts
Her emotionally.
And I--I dream to touch her,
I dream to make her fantasies our realities.
I dream to be her knight,
Who rides her off into the sunset and follow the
Stars that shine at night.
I dream to make her minds fantasies
Into her eyes realities...
I dream--to touch her...

Martice S. Hanible

Date: 5-10-07
Place: Danville C.C.
Time: 5:47 P.M.
Reason: For my guy John-John (ya-ya) as a response to his girl Tajwana poem.
Inspiration: My guys girl poem "Never Been Touched".

Today I Vow

You know when I first laid eyes on you, I was
Kind of mesmerized. And I wondered why, would
God create such a goddess for another man, but not
For me.
I smiled at you and I joked with you, but deep down
Inside I still wondered why.
As time went on I--I admired in you the attributes
That any man would love to have in his goddess.
But now--now I have you standing here next to me
With your hand embedded in mine. And today I--I vow
To protect the very core of your being—your essence.

(name), today I vow to protect every
Strand of your emotional being. To never take
For granted your tears of joy and to never make
You cry tears of unhappiness.

(name), today I vow to love you the way
You want to be loved. For you deserve to be loved
The way the sun should love the moon, the way the
Ocean should love the sand, the way an African
King should love his African Queen.

(name), today I vow to try and understand
Your every dream, your every thought,
Your every desire. To understand your past, your
Experiences, your passions, your goals. For your
Past is now my past, your today is my today, and
Together our future sits in heaven already
Written and etched in gold.

(name), today I vow to love you every-
Single-day, with every morsel of strength that
I have in my being. For my every days' journey will
Be to make you happy. And my every seconds' enjoyment
Will be that of learning how.

Martice S. Hanible

(<u>name</u>), this I vow.

Date: 5-15-07
Place: Danville C.C.
Time: 3:10 P.M.
Reason: My manz Rob about to get married.
Inspiration: I always wanted to write something on this, but my guy decision gave me inspiration, hopefully he'll use it as his actual vows.

Dear Young Madre

Dear young Madre,
Through the eyes of the Incas
Through the artistry of the Aztecs
Through the textiles of the Toltecs
And through the architecture of the Olmecs
You have been the birthright of it all.

Through the jubilations of cultural survival
Through the attempts to make distinct the indigenous
Through the resurrections and revolutions
Through the unjustified resolutions of the constitution
And through those inequitable and still unresolved American Restitutions
Your life has fed the rebirth of the strength to survive it all.

Through the constant migrating of an unjustifiably misplaced
Human family,
Through the fields across America as a workplace
Through the strawberry hills of a father and mother trying to provide
For their son and daughters
Through racism, disenfranchisement and street hustles
And through the academic and redlining prejudices
You--yours Madre-- carry within your soul the potential
To give birth to those who will recreate a new heaven
A new earth...
And we celebrate that potential on this Happy Mothers' Day...
"Alegre Madre Dia"

Date: 5-05-08
Place: Danville C.C. 4B-16
Reason: For Rina for Mothers' Day Inspiration: Rina

Stand Strong Princess

We sit when we stand princess,
We crawl when we can't walk.
We fight haplessly when we're not strong,
And we fight relentlessly to become strong.
We forget our strengths at times,
So we forget how strong we truly are.
We forget how much we've already faced in life,
And how we've overcome it all.
We forget how hard it was to smile even though
We were sad,
We forget how we defeated our downfall, and how
We made a success out of our jagged past.
Princess sometimes....
We simply forget the strength we have.
So stand strong princess,
And hold your head high.
For this too will be another victory that you've overcome.
And always remember princess...
That when you can't stand on your own,
You'll always have my shoulders to lean on.
Therefore you'll always be standing strong.

Date: 3-17-07
Place: Danville C.C.
Reason: For a birthday (Mustafa) family member in hospital.

As a Man Thinketh

I want me an Alicia Keys,
A Michelle Obama,
An Angela Bassette,
An Angelina Jolie,
A Rosie Perez...
I want a woman who has the ability to think beyond herself
And desire to be more than a fashion side show,
Or recipient of love only when life's good.
I want a woman who has the strength to hold me down
When life's tight,
And things not right.
Be a mother to a child
While being a scholar to another,
And a comforter to the world.
I'm just looking for a woman
Who's a sweetheart in her life,
But strong enough to hold her own.
I need an Alicia Keys,
A Michelle Obama,
An Angela Bassette,
An Angelina Jolie,
A Rosie Perez...

Place: Hill C.C. 2C-66
Date: 6-28-09
Inspiration: Alicial Keys received her Humanitarian Award on BET
6-28-09

To My Extended Essence

How are you doing baby?
I'm just sitting here lonely and thinking about you, (as I always do)
It's crazy how things can change a man to make him desire what
He once had, but he never at that moment cherished. It's crazy
How reality can make a man submit to his natural nature and
Crave to live within and exude his natural elements. They say,
"Time will change a man; for with time comes knowledge".
But I say, "Experience will change a man; for from experience
Comes understanding and appreciation". For a man never
Knows himself--until he experiences who he is not. For
Man never knew there was a law--until man violated the
Laws of nature.
It is pertinent that man not be by himself, for he was not made to be
alone. For man in this era journeys on a path of loneliness, unaware of
his natural nature and defiling his extended essence; woman.
For a man and his desires, experiences loneliness as his conclusion. And I
princess, will love to experience happiness as mines...so I...I need you to
love you....

Love, Martice

Date: 3-16-07
Place: Danville C.C.
Reason: A letter to Rina Hernandez
Inspiration: Just a thought while writing a letter...

Before I Pass Away

Before I cross through the portals of the other
Realm of life that some call death,
And travel through the light that others call heaven.
Before I walk through the doors of the first heaven,
To walk into the gates of the 7th.
Before my spirit is weighed by Maat, the goddess of
Justice and Righteousness,
And my form is transformed for a limited amount
Of time.
I just wanted you to know...that I love you...

Before my breath is taken away from me,
And my heart beats it's final drum,
Before I lay unawake in the physical form,
And my body lay stable without movable pace.
Before I pass away,
And leave you here on God's green earth.
I just wanted you to know...that I love you...

Date: 4-04-08
Time: 11:59 P.M.
Place: Danville C.C. 4B-16
Inspiration: Watching Tyra Banks show with Alicia Keys as a guest
Alicia sings "Like I'll Never See You Again".

Why Does She Fear

Why does she fear when she's great?
When she's more than great, when she's the
World's fate.
When she's an angel walking on solid
Ground.
When she's so wonderful that she makes
God jealous that she walks among us
And not among the clouds.
When she's everything a man could ever
Wish for,
When she's beautiful, intelligent, playful,
And strong.

Why does she fear when things start
To go right?
When God walks into her life,
And makes it all right.
Why does she fear success and feel
Unworthy of her own greatness?
When she, as a seed, already housed the
Potential in her DNA that she has learned
To manifest to become Rina Hernandez.
Why does she fear?

Date: 5-30-07
Place: Danville C.C.
Time: 8:57 P.M.
Inspiration: A letter from Rina Hernandez saying that she fear.

Lonely Nights and Saddened Days

Lonely nights and saddened days
 In a place where thoughts
Of companionship are
Thoughts mentally contained;
That you can't escape.

Dreams and wishes of
The queens and misses;
That you never entertained
But you wish that you
Would've

Scores of memories
Of past loves and
Sexy nights;
Even reminiscent of past
Premonitions of
What you once proudly did
Wrong
That you will now earnestly
Do right.

Ideas of future loves
Do's and won'ts
Maybes and mights;
Yearnings for the inner
Beauty of a princess that
Is pertinent as the
Ultimate quality
In a future wife.

Lonely nights and saddened days
Where you sit silently
Thinking and you gaze
That...you never would
Have in the days were...

Martice S. Hanible

Love was not essential
And life didn't include a
Her.

But as the pain hits
And the tears in a
Growing mans eyes stir;
Maturity seems to come
Into existence and
Your true nature as a man
Begins to exert.

Where the stomach turns
And knots in your throat
Grow;
Because you're now
Missing what you never
Imagined would at any
Time be of importance to
Your ego...
That...which is now essentially
Called ...Her.

In these lonely nights and these
saddened days...
Where you sit silently

Date: April 2, 2010
Place: Statesville C.C. F338
Reason: Bored
Inspiration: My celly (Treon) feeling it today.

I Never Knew Who You Were (Until I Lost You)

I never knew who you were until I lost you,
I learned that diamonds and gold are comparable, but you are an
Incomparable jewel,
Princess, you are comparable to nothing and no one.
Time cannot fly back in order for me to appreciate
What I had.
I had an intellectual dime,
A woman who was ambitiously fine
A courageous human being with a strong inner mind,
A woman who's the apple to any man's eye.
But I didn't appreciate you,
I didn't appreciate you,
Because I never knew who you were until I lost you.

You are the most gorgeous woman I've ever seen,
The greatest woman that I've ever been around,
You are my soul-mate, my lost--my found.
You are the answer to my every question.
My destiny to my quest,
My completion to my happiness.
Baby, you are my jewel,
But I never knew who you were until I lost you...

Date: 7-22-07
Time: 1:54 P.M.
Inspiration: T.V. show Baio 45 and single going around apologizing to old girlfriends who was good to him, but he dogged out.
To: Art of Noise "special kind of fool (for you)"

Open Your Heart (and Let Me Enter)

Baby, open your heart
And let me enter,
Let me have the opportunity
To mend the shattered vessels
That carries your love
From you to me---
Let me be the man who
Appreciates what you bring
As a human being,
And offers as a companion,
And gives as a woman.

Let me be the inspiration
That makes you smile…
The endorphin that relaxes
Every single cornel of Your being
And every single hurt of
Your life (soul).

Baby, open your heart
And let me enter,
Let me live where you've
Walled off to all others,
And dwell where you feel
Will be trampled.
Let me lounge where
Others have lived as
Temporary tenants,
Who had no intentions
Of permanently housing
Themselves there
Because as nomads
They had no desire
To live other than vagabonds.

Baby, open your heart

To Kiss The Soul Of A Woman

And let me enter,
Let me be the healer
That you never thought
Existed
That diagnosis that
Offers hope of a better
Prognosis
That patient homebuilder
That chips away at the
Mortared brick that you've
Used to wall off your
Greatest asset.
Let me be to you
What I want you to be to
Me…
Baby…
Let me be your heaven…

Date: April 3, 2010
Place: Statesville C.C. F-338
Inspiration: Just thinking about women whose heart is walled off because of past heart breaks.

I Came to Restore You

She thinks every man comes for one thing,
She thinks a man could only love her body and not her
Mind; not her soul.
She's afraid to love, cause she's afraid of pain,
She's afraid of man, because of her past.
She has placed me on the level that she's placed all men,
She's afraid to fall in love with me, because she's afraid
To take the chance.
To take the chance of me hurting her heart,
She's afraid to take the chance of me not loving her soul.
She's afraid of man, but she shouldn't be afraid of me,
But she has to understand me.
She has to understand that I am the essence of man,
Not the replication of her past (man).
She has to know that, I come not to hurt her,
But to love her.
To love her...
To restore her...

Date: 7-16-07
Place: Danville C.C.
Time: 1:37 P.M.
Inspiration: Tyler Perry movie "Family Reunion".
To: Isley brothers "Hello (or) Don't Change"

Will She Ever Have the Chance To Love Her Soul mate...

Will she ever be happy loving who she's loving,
When she's knowing
That who she's loving
Is not really who she wants to love.
She's constantly wondering about her feelings and her
Dreams,
She's constantly thinking about how true love really feels.
She's dreaming of times she's never had,
And things she has yet to feel.
She thinks about her soul mate, her true complement,
And cries because she can't be with him,
So she drowns in her own tears.
She echoes his name when no one is around, so that no one
Could hear her,
Without him loving her, she's not content, she's not
Happy, she's just living.
She has continued to go through life living and loving
Who she's loving diligently,
But with false commitment,
She knows her body is her lover's sacrament,
But her heart and her mind belongs to her compliment.
She's in love with an image that she physically can't have,
She has to sacrifice her heart, because of the obstacles of
The world.
She's learned now that love hurts,
But through loving her complement, she's experienced
That love's real.
But will she ever...Have the chance... to fall in
Love...or to love...her soul mate...

Date: 09-06-07
Place: Danville C.C.
Inspiration: A letter Rina wrote me 8-16-07 and I received 9-04-07 telling me my incarceration hinders us from going further and being more than friends.
To: One way "Guess You Didn't Know (that I Loved You).

Finding Our 7th Heaven

I know we have met before,
Somewhere, we were once in love.
Maybe you were my dream girl,
Way beyond the bonds of our green earth.
Maybe we were husband and wife, in another Life
Maybe we were a bond of excellence shinning
In a perfect light.

(name), I'm not for sure,
But I know we have met somewhere before...
Our hearts were destined to meet one another,
For some strange reason, they simultaneously beat
With a synchronized rhythm.
Our words are spoken with a familiar accent,
Our communications are pleasant, with one of us
Finishing the other's sentences.

(name), I'm not for sure,
But I know we have met somewhere before
Did I travel from heaven to heaven to find
You once more?
Did you travel from earth to land to find me
Again?
Did we search each plain of life, until we've
Finally found one another?
Did we scramble through troubled relationships
To find our 7th Heaven?

(name), I' not for sure,
But I know we have met somewhere before....

Date: 2-14-08
Place: Danville C.C. 4B-16
Inspiration: Just saw "Prince" newly released video, "Somewhere Here on Earth", and I thought about what Rina told me in one of her letters, a couple months ago; "I think we were married in another life"..

May I Kiss Those Tears Away

Princess, may I kiss those tears away?
May I gently hold your hands
And tell you I understand
That--men have failed to comprehend,
The incalculable value of a woman.
I've seen men talk down to you,
I've seen men physically abuse you.
I've seen men act nice to you,
Just to make love to you.
I've heard men tell you
That they love you when they didn't,
They tried to use you for their
Personal benefit.
I've seen men marry you
Just to use, abuse, try to change
And control you,
And then the man
After you bore his child--left you
Because truthfully--he never
Had any intentions on ever
Loving either one of you two.
But you have to be the true princess,
You have to be strong
And move on
Without holding every man responsible
For the wrong doings of another man.
You have to look at me as being me
And put me on my own level.
You have to let me love you,
The way I know how to.
And let me learn to treat you
The way you want me to.
I can't erase your past, Princess--,
But I can erase the pain.
I could make you feel that every
Love song is your story,

And feel that every love poem
Is your autobiography.
I could let you know that you are
Worth more to me,
Than every breath I breathe...
That you are more valuable to me,
Than every--single--heartbeat.
For you were made for me...from me,
For you are what protects my heartbeat...
For you are my rib,
My greatest asset.
So I sit here and I bear witness to your
Tears rolling down those gorgeous cheeks,
I just had to ask...
Baby;
May I kiss those tears away?

Date: 11-17-06
Place: Stateville C.C.
Inspiration: A leter from Rina

I Just Want to Make Love to You

I just want to make love to you.
Baby, I just want to do to you the things your man wouldn't do.
Cut your steaks for you, and feed fruit to you,
Talk sex talk with you, just to learn what you want a man
To do to you.

Baby, I just want to make love to you.
Talk with you to make you smile,
Smile with you to make you laugh,
Reach across the table to hold your hands,
Kiss your palms while looking into your eyes.

Baby, I just want to make love to you.
Take our time to walk down Lakeshore Drive,
And while talking, I could admire the moon which is the
Reflection I see in your eyes.
Place my hands around your waist and rub down your
Hips to your outer thighs.

Baby, I just want to make love to you,
And walk down to Buckingham Fountain,
Take pictures with the back of my pointer finger casually
Strolling down the sides of your cheeks.

Let the drizzles of the rain dampen and wet you,
And before you go home, allow me to gently hug and
Compassionately kiss you.
Because tonight, Baby, I didn't want to have sex with you--
I just wanted to make love to you.

Date 7-27-07
Place: Danville C.C.
Time: 8:02 P.M.
Inspiration: None, just thinking/wrote.
Reason: None just writing to O'Jays "We Cry Together".

About The Author

Martice Hanible is the eldest son and has four siblings; he is also the father to one daughter.

Martice was inherently born a gentleman from the lineage of his father and both grandfathers but his life spiraled out of control in his teen years and he found himself incarcerated in 1996 at the age of 20. Sentenced to 80 years, Martice is due to be released in 2026.

Martice says that prison has not hardened him; it has made him stronger and more appreciative of life and has served as the mechanism that has helped him find his true self and his true passion in life – writing.

You may write Martice directly at:

> Martice S. Hanible #K70069
> Hill Correctional Center
> POBox 1700
> Galesburg IL 61402

Martice S. Hanible

Midnight Express Books

Name: _____

Address: _____

City: _____ State: _____ Zip: _____

____ To Kiss the Soul of a Woman $12.95

            ____ **Total number of books ordered**   Subtotal ____

Shipping/Handling
First book $3.95
Each additional book   add $1.50*

                                                    Total S/H ____

                                      TOTAL ENCLOSED ____

This offer for a limited time

Send check or money order (no cash or stamps) to:

**Midnight Express Books
POBox 69
Berryville AR 72616**

Additional books may be purchased from MidnightExpressbooks.com; Inmatebooks@yahoo.com (accepts stamps); Amazon.com; and any other place where books are sold.

To Kiss The Soul Of A Woman

www.ingramcontent.com/pod-product-compliance
Lightning Source LLC
Chambersburg PA
CBHW072014060426
42446CB00043B/2546